The Rabbit and the Turnip

LEVEL B

A Publication of the World Language Division

Editor-in-Chief: Judith Bittinger

Project Director: Elinor Chamas

Editorial Development: Elly Schottman

Production/Manufacturing: James W. Gibbons

Cover and Text Design/Art Direction: Taurins Design
Associates, New York

Illustrator: Frank Bozzo

ISBN 0-201-19360-4
10 11 12-WR-96 95 94

Addison-Wesley Publishing Company

Reading, Massachusetts • Menlo Park, California • New York • Don Mills, Ontario • Wokingham, England
Amsterdam • Bonn • Sydney • Singapore • Tokyo • Madrid • San Juan

It was winter.
It was snowing very hard.
It was very cold.

The animals were out
looking for food.

4

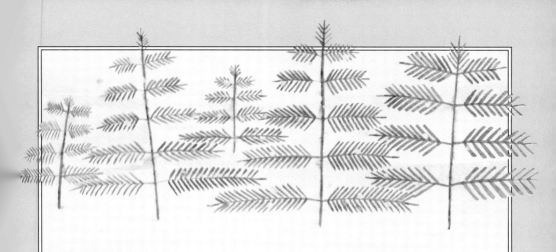

Little Rabbit found two turnips. He gobbled one right up. He wanted the other turnip. Then he thought about his friend Little Donkey.

"Little Donkey is probably hungry, too. I'll take this turnip to him." Little Donkey was not at home. Little Rabbit left the turnip on his doorstep.

Little Donkey came home. He had some potatoes to eat. He was very surprised to see the turnip. "How kind of someone to give me this turnip," he thought.

8

"Little Sheep is probably hungry, too. I'll take this turnip to her." Little Sheep was not at home.
Little Donkey left the turnip on her table.

Little Sheep came home. She had a cabbage to eat. She was very surprised to see the turnip. "How kind of someone to give me this turnip," she thought.

"Little Doe is probably hungry, too. I'll take this turnip to her." Little Doe was not at home. Little Sheep left the turnip on her windowsill.

Little Doe came home. She had some leaves to eat. She was very surprised to see the turnip. "How kind of someone to give me this turnip," she thought.

12

"Little Rabbit is probably hungry, too. I'll take this turnip to him." Little Rabbit was at home. He was fast asleep. Little Doe left the turnip beside his bed.

Little Rabbit woke up.
He was very surprised to see the turnip.
He thought he was dreaming.

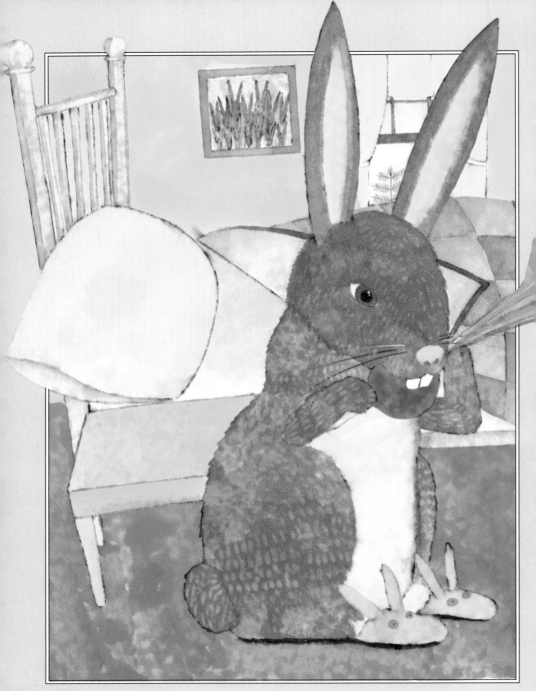

"How kind of someone to give me this turnip," he thought. And he gobbled it right up.

The End